LITERARY FIRST AID KIT

LITERARY FIRST AID KIT

Summersdale Publishers Ltd
46 West Street
Chichester
West Sussex
PO19 1RP
UK

www.summersdale.com

Printed and bound in the Czech Republic

ISBN: 978-1-84953-733-9

Substantial discounts on bulk quantities of Summersdale books are available to corporations, professional associations and other organisations. For details contact Nicky Douglas by telephone: +44 (0) 1243 756902, fax: +44 (0) 1243 786300 or email: nicky@summersdale.com.

LITERARY FIRST AID KIT

Words for Everyday Dilemmas, Decisions and Emergencies

ABBIE HEADON

summersdale

To Mum, Dad and James, for raising a bookworm, and to Jeremy, for marrying one

CONTENTS

INTRODUCTION

Why do we love books? I think the answer lies in the fact that when we dive into a book, we enter another world and leave the cares of our own lives behind for a while. Books can take us to places we'll never go, from Sauron's Dark Tower to the Hundred Acre Wood, from the age of the dinosaurs to the twenty-fifth century, from the grinding poverty of Victorian London to the most extravagant excesses of the Sun King's court at Versailles.

Through reading books, we come to know how people tick. We meet braggers and bullies, saints and sinners, lovers and liars – and we recognise aspects of ourselves in all of them. When a character grieves or rejoices, we learn vicariously what it's like to experience those emotions. Books allow us to get inside the minds of misfits and oddballs, and to forgive ourselves for our failings. We watch characters succeed and fail, and we see how their lives unfold, whether as a result of their actions or simply of blind chance.

In this *Literary First Aid Kit*, I've endeavoured to bring together the most inspiring, comforting and reassuring extracts from well-known books, in a longer-form follow-up to my *Poetry First Aid Kit*. While I was researching this book I revisited many old favourites of mine to dig out their most cheering literary nuggets, such as the time in Jerome K. Jerome's *Three Men in a Boat* when the narrator looks up his symptoms in the British Library and ends up diagnosing himself with everything except housemaid's knee, and I made lots of new discoveries as well, led on a page-hopping journey from book to book by recommendations from friends and family, and by the sheer luck of stumbling upon new gems in the bookshelves.

In this selection of literary excerpts, I hope you'll find ingredients to cheer and console you. You can search through chapters that relate to whatever is worrying you at the moment, or simply dip in at random to see what cure your heart leads you to, whether it's the key to a decorating dilemma or a possible answer to one of life's big questions.

As the old song has it, 'Love is good for anything that ails you' – but after a course of literary first aid, I hope you'll agree with me that books are just what the doctor ordered, every time.

I'd love to hear your literary prescriptions, too – drop me a line via Twitter and let me know how the medicine went down, at @AbbieHeadon.

Abbie Headon, 2015

EVERYDAY
LIFE

If your friends don't understand just how important your dog is to you:

And can we, without the basest ingratitude, think ill of an animal, that has ever honoured mankind with his company and friendship, from the beginning of the world to the present moment? While all other creatures are in a state of enmity with us; some flying into woods and wildernesses to escape our tyranny, and others requiring to be restrained with bridles and fences in close confinement; dogs alone enter into voluntary friendship with us, and of their own accord make their residence among us.

Francis Coventry, *The History of Pompey the Little*

If you find yourself feeling envious of other people:

The Peacock was greatly discontented because he had not a beautiful voice like the nightingale, and he went and complained to Juno about it. 'The nightingale's song,' said he, 'is the envy of all the birds; but whenever I utter a sound I become a laughing-stock.' The goddess tried to console him by saying, 'You have not, it is true, the power of song, but then you far excel all the rest in beauty: your neck flashes like the emerald and your splendid tail is a marvel of gorgeous colour.' But the Peacock was not appeased. 'What is the use,' said he, 'of being beautiful, with a voice like mine?' Then Juno replied, with a shade of sternness in her tones, 'Fate has allotted to all their destined gifts: to yourself beauty, to the eagle strength, to the nightingale song, and so on to all the rest in their degree; but you alone are dissatisfied with your portion. Make, then, no more complaints. For, if your present wish were granted, you would quickly find cause for fresh discontent.'

Aesop, *Aesop's Fables*

If you are wondering how best to dispose of a gloriously sunny afternoon:

Under certain circumstances there are few hours in life more agreeable than the hour dedicated to the ceremony known as afternoon tea. There are circumstances in which, whether you partake of the tea or not – some people of course never do, – the situation is in itself delightful. Those that I have in mind in beginning to unfold this simple history offered an admirable setting to an innocent pastime. The implements of the little feast had been disposed upon the lawn of an old English country-house, in what I should call the perfect middle of a splendid summer afternoon. Part of the afternoon had waned, but much of it was left, and what was left was of the finest and rarest quality. Real dusk would not arrive for many hours; but the flood of summer light had begun to ebb, the air had grown mellow, the shadows were long upon the smooth, dense turf. They lengthened slowly, however, and the scene expressed that sense of leisure still to come which is perhaps the chief source of one's enjoyment of such a scene at such an hour. From five o'clock to eight is on certain occasions a little eternity; but on such an occasion as this the interval could be only an eternity of pleasure.

Henry James, *The Portrait of a Lady*

If you need to find a diplomatic way to tell somebody their table manners are not quite up to scratch:

We had made some progress in the dinner, when I reminded Herbert of his promise to tell me about Miss Havisham.

'True,' he replied. 'I'll redeem it at once. Let me introduce the topic, Handel, by mentioning that in London it is not the custom to put the knife in the mouth – for fear of accidents – and that while the fork is reserved for that use, it is not put further in than necessary. It is scarcely worth mentioning, only it's as well to do as other people do. Also, the spoon is not generally used over-hand, but under. This has two advantages. You get at your mouth better (which after all is the object), and you save a good deal of the attitude of opening oysters, on the part of the right elbow.'

He offered these friendly suggestions in such a lively way, that we both laughed and I scarcely blushed.

Charles Dickens, *Great Expectations*

If you are considering making your rooms look bigger by hanging lots of mirrors on the walls:

The rage for glitter – because its idea has become as we before observed, confounded with that of magnificence in the abstract – has led us, also, to the exaggerated employment of mirrors. We line our dwellings with great British plates, and then imagine we have done a fine thing. Now the slightest thought will be sufficient to convince any one who has an eye at all, of the ill effect of numerous looking glasses, and especially of large ones. Regarded apart from its reflection, the mirror presents a continuous, flat, colourless, unrelieved surface, – a thing always and obviously unpleasant. Considered as a reflector, it is potent in producing a monstrous and odious uniformity: and the evil is here aggravated, not in merely direct proportion with the augmentation of its sources, but in a ratio constantly increasing. In fact, a room with four or five mirrors arranged at random, is, for all purposes of artistic show, a room of no shape at all. If we add to this evil, the attendant glitter upon glitter, we have a perfect farrago of discordant and displeasing effects. The veriest bumpkin, on entering an apartment so bedizzened, would be instantly aware of something wrong, although he might be altogether unable to assign a cause for his dissatisfaction.

Edgar Allan Poe, 'The Philosophy of Furniture'

If you need a plausible excuse to free yourself from unwanted social engagements:

ALGERNON: What you really are is a Bunburyist. I was quite right in saying you were a Bunburyist. You are one of the most advanced Bunburyists I know.

JACK: What on earth do you mean?

ALGERNON: You have invented a very useful younger brother called Ernest, in order that you may be able to come up to town as often as you like. I have invented an invaluable permanent invalid called Bunbury, in order that I may be able to go down into the country whenever I choose. Bunbury is perfectly invaluable. If it wasn't for Bunbury's extraordinary bad health, for instance, I wouldn't be able to dine with you at Willis's to-night, for I have been really engaged to Aunt Augusta for more than a week.

Oscar Wilde, *The Importance of Being Earnest*

If you need to fend off unwanted physical advances:

The benign and fatherly old man put his arm round her waist. Fresh from the tonic of pure air, and with the notion of his ridiculousness still in her mind, she was staggered for an instant by this gesture. She had never given a thought to the temperament of the old grocer, the husband of a young wife. She could not always imaginatively keep in mind the effect of her own radiance, especially under such circumstances. But after an instant her precocious cynicism, which had slept, sprang up. 'Naturally! I might have expected it!' she thought with blasting scorn.

'Take away your hand!' she said bitterly to the amiable old fool. She did not stir.

He obeyed, sheepishly.

Arnold Bennett, *The Old Wives' Tale*

If you are concerned about how to maintain good friendships:

Friendship can only be bred in practice and be maintained by practice. Affection, nay, love itself, is no help at all to friendship. True, active, productive friendship consists in keeping equal pace in life: in my friend approving my aims, while I approve his, and in thus moving forwards together steadfastly, however much our way of thought and life may vary.

Johann Wolfgang von Goethe,
Maxims and Reflections

If you worry that you don't have the gift of the gab:

People in general attach too much importance to words. They are under the illusion that talking effects great results. As a matter of fact, words are, as a rule, the shallowest portion of all the argument. They but dimly represent the great surging feelings and desires which lie behind. When the distraction of the tongue is removed, the heart listens.

Theodore Dreiser, *Sister Carrie*

If everything is going wrong and you are finding it hard to look on the bright side:

'Well, this is wonderful!' said Candide, 'but you must get cured.'

'Alas! how can I?' said Pangloss, 'I have not a farthing, my friend, and all over the globe there is no letting of blood or taking a glister, without paying, or somebody paying for you.'

These last words determined Candide; he went and flung himself at the feet of the charitable Anabaptist James, and gave him so touching a picture of the state to which his friend was reduced, that the good man did not scruple to take Dr Pangloss into his house, and had him cured at his expense. In the cure Pangloss lost only an eye and an ear. He wrote well, and knew arithmetic perfectly. The Anabaptist James made him his bookkeeper. At the end of two months, being obliged to go to Lisbon about some mercantile affairs, he took the two philosophers with him in his ship. Pangloss explained to him how everything was so constituted that it could not be better.

[...]

'All this was indispensable,' replied the one-eyed doctor, 'for private misfortunes make the general good, so that the more private misfortunes there are the greater is the general good.'

Voltaire, *Candide*

If you are embarrassed about admitting to your superstitions:

In spite of hosts of deniers, and asserters, and wise-men, and professors, the majority still are averse to sitting down to dine thirteen at table, or being helped to salt, or walking under a ladder, or seeing a single magpie flirting his chequered tail. There are, of course, children of light who have set their faces against all this, though even a newspaper man, if you entice him into a cemetery at midnight, will believe in phantoms, for everyone is a visionary, if you scratch him deep enough.

William Butler Yeats, from the Introduction to *Fairy and Folk Tales of the Irish Peasantry*

HEALTH AND BEAUTY

If you are wondering whether to take up exercise:

In Meryton they parted; the two youngest repaired to the lodgings of one of the officers' wives, and Elizabeth continued her walk alone, crossing field after field at a quick pace, jumping over stiles and springing over puddles with impatient activity, and finding herself at last within view of the house, with weary ankles, dirty stockings, and a face glowing with the warmth of exercise.

She was shown into the breakfast-parlour, where all but Jane were assembled, and where her appearance created a great deal of surprise. That she should have walked three miles so early in the day, in such dirty weather, and by herself, was almost incredible to Mrs Hurst and Miss Bingley; and Elizabeth was convinced that they held her in contempt for it. She was received, however, very politely by them; and in their brother's manners there was something better than politeness; there was good humour and kindness. Mr Darcy said very little, and Mr Hurst nothing at all. The former was divided between admiration of the brilliancy which exercise had given to her complexion, and doubt as to the occasion's justifying her coming so far alone. The latter was thinking only of his breakfast.

Jane Austen, *Pride and Prejudice*

If you are feeling under the weather and you decide to research your symptoms on the Internet:

I remember going to the British Museum one day to read up the treatment for some slight ailment of which I had a touch – hay fever, I fancy it was. I got down the book, and read all I came to read; and then, in an unthinking moment, I idly turned the leaves, and began to indolently study diseases, generally. I forget which was the first distemper I plunged into – some fearful, devastating scourge, I know – and, before I had glanced half down the list of 'premonitory symptoms', it was borne in upon me that I had fairly got it.

I sat for awhile, frozen with horror; and then, in the listlessness of despair, I again turned over the pages. I came to typhoid fever – read the symptoms – discovered that I had typhoid fever, must have had it for months without knowing it – wondered what else I had got; turned up St. Vitus's Dance – found, as I expected, that I had that too, – began to get interested in my case, and determined to sift it to the bottom, and so started alphabetically – read up ague, and learnt that I was sickening for it, and that the acute stage would commence in about another fortnight. Bright's disease, I was relieved to find, I had only in a modified form, and, so far as that was concerned, I might live for years. Cholera I had, with severe complications; and diphtheria I seemed to have been born with. I plodded conscientiously through the twenty-six letters, and the only malady I could conclude I had not got was housemaid's knee.

I felt rather hurt about this at first; it seemed somehow to be a sort of slight. Why hadn't I got housemaid's knee? Why this invidious reservation? After a while, however, less grasping feelings prevailed. I reflected that I had every other known malady in the pharmacology, and I grew less selfish, and determined to do without housemaid's knee. Gout, in its most malignant stage, it would appear, had seized me without my being aware of it; and zymosis I had evidently been suffering with from boyhood. There were no more diseases after zymosis, so I concluded there was nothing else the matter with me.

Jerome K. Jerome, *Three Men in a Boat*

If you are considering the joys of a low-carb diet:

When the girl returned, some hours later, she carried a tray, with a cup of fragrant tea steaming on it; and a plate piled up with very hot buttered toast, cut thick, very brown on both sides, with the butter running through the holes in great golden drops, like honey from the honeycomb. The smell of that buttered toast simply talked to Toad, and with no uncertain voice; talked of warm kitchens, of breakfasts on bright frosty mornings, of cosy parlour firesides on winter evenings, when one's ramble was over and slippered feet were propped on the fender, of the purring of contented cats, and the twitter of sleepy canaries.

Kenneth Grahame, *The Wind in the Willows*

If you think your mind might be playing tricks on you:

'You don't believe in me,' observed the Ghost.

'I don't,' said Scrooge.

'What evidence would you have of my reality beyond that of your senses?'

'I don't know,' said Scrooge.

'Why do you doubt your senses?'

'Because,' said Scrooge, 'a little thing affects them. A slight disorder of the stomach makes them cheats. You may be an undigested bit of beef, a blot of mustard, a crumb of cheese, a fragment of an underdone potato. There's more of gravy than of grave about you, whatever you are!'

Charles Dickens, *A Christmas Carol*

If you are looking for a simple way to keep your mind alert and active:

I cannot forbear to mention among these precepts a new device for study which, although it may seem but trivial and almost ludicrous, is nevertheless extremely useful in arousing the mind to various inventions. And this is, when you look at a wall spotted with stains, or with a mixture of stones, if you have to devise some scene, you may discover a resemblance to various landscapes, beautified with mountains, rivers, rocks, trees, plains, wide valleys and hills in varied arrangement; or again you may see battles and figures in action; or strange faces and costumes, and an endless variety of objects, which you could reduce to complete and well drawn forms. And these appear on such walls confusedly, like the sound of bells in whose jangle you may find any name or word you choose to imagine.

Leonardo da Vinci, *The Notebooks of Leonardo da Vinci*

If you worry that you don't look 'perfect' enough:

As therefore the sweetest rose hath his prickle, the finest velvet his brack, the fairest flower his bran, so the sharpest wit hath his wanton will, and the holiest head his wicked way. And true it is that some men write and most men believe, that in all perfect shapes, a blemish bringeth rather a liking every way to the eyes, than a loathing any way to the mind. Venus had her mole in her cheek which made her more amiable: Helen her scar on her chin which Paris called *cos amoris*, the whetstone of love.

John Lyly, *Euphues: The Anatomy of Wit*

If you are considering economising by dyeing your own hair:

'Anne Shirley, whatever is the matter with you? What have you done? Get right up this minute and tell me. This minute, I say. There now, what is it?'

Anne had slid to the floor in despairing obedience.

'Look at my hair, Marilla,' she whispered.

Accordingly, Marilla lifted her candle and looked scrutinisingly at Anne's hair, flowing in heavy masses down her back. It certainly had a very strange appearance.

'Anne Shirley, what have you done to your hair? Why, it's GREEN!'

Green it might be called, if it were any earthly colour – a queer, dull, bronzy green, with streaks here and there of the original red to heighten the ghastly effect. Never in all her life had Marilla seen anything so grotesque as Anne's hair at that moment.

'Yes, it's green,' moaned Anne. 'I thought nothing could be as bad as red hair. But now I know it's ten times worse to have green hair. Oh, Marilla, you little know how utterly wretched I am.'

35

'I little know how you got into this fix, but I mean to find out,' said Marilla. 'Come right down to the kitchen – it's too cold up here – and tell me just what you've done. I've been expecting something queer for some time. You haven't got into any scrape for over two months, and I was sure another one was due. Now, then, what did you do to your hair?'

'I dyed it.'

'Dyed it! Dyed your hair! Anne Shirley, didn't you know it was a wicked thing to do?'

'Yes, I knew it was a little wicked,' admitted Anne. 'But I thought it was worth while to be a little wicked to get rid of red hair. I counted the cost, Marilla. Besides, I meant to be extra good in other ways to make up for it.'

'Well,' said Marilla sarcastically, 'if I'd decided it was worth while to dye my hair I'd have dyed it a decent colour at least. I wouldn't have dyed it green.'

'But I didn't mean to dye it green, Marilla,' protested Anne dejectedly. 'If I was wicked I meant to be wicked to some purpose. He said it would turn my hair a beautiful raven black – he positively assured me that it would. How could I doubt his word, Marilla?'

L. M. Montgomery, *Anne of Green Gables*

If you are lying awake at night planning exactly what to wear for a big event:

Dress is at all times a frivolous distinction, and excessive solicitude about it often destroys its own aim. Catherine knew all this very well; her great aunt had read her a lecture on the subject only the Christmas before; and yet she lay awake ten minutes on Wednesday night debating between her spotted and her tamboured muslin, and nothing but the shortness of the time prevented her buying a new one for the evening. This would have been an error in judgment, great though not uncommon, from which one of the other sex rather than her own, a brother rather than a great aunt, might have warned her, for man only can be aware of the insensibility of man towards a new gown. It would be mortifying to the feelings of many ladies, could they be made to understand how little the heart of man is affected by what is costly or new in their attire; how little it is biased by the texture of their muslin, and how unsusceptible of peculiar tenderness towards the spotted, the sprigged, the mull, or the jackonet. Woman is fine for her own satisfaction alone. No man will admire her the more, no woman will like her the better for it. Neatness and fashion are enough for the former, and a something of shabbiness or impropriety will be most endearing to the latter.

Jane Austen, *Northanger Abbey*

LIFE'S
TEMPTATIONS

If you feel obliged to have just a little sip of alcohol, for medicinal purposes, and no more than that:

'If it wasn't for the nerve a little sip of liquor gives me (I never was able to do more than taste it), I never could go through with what I sometimes has to do. "Mrs Harris," I says, at the very last case as ever I acted in, which it was but a young person, "Mrs Harris," I says, "leave the bottle on the chimley-piece, and don't ask me to take none, but let me put my lips to it when I am so disposed, and then I will do what I'm engaged to do, according to the best of my ability." "Mrs Gamp," she says, in answer, "if ever there was a sober creetur to be got at eighteen pence a day for working people, and three and six for gentlefolks – night watching,"' said Mrs Gamp with emphasis, '"being a extra charge – you are that inwallable person." "Mrs Harris," I says to her, "don't name the charge, for if I could afford to lay all my feller creeturs out for nothink, I would gladly do it, sich is the love I bears 'em. But what I always says to them as has the management of matters, Mrs

Harris'" – here she kept her eye on Mr Pecksniff – "'be they gents or be they ladies, is, don't ask me whether I won't take none, or whether I will, but leave the bottle on the chimley-piece, and let me put my lips to it when I am so dispoged.'"

Charles Dickens, *Martin Chuzzlewit*

If you have thought of an excellent joke about your friends, and you're tempted to share it with them:

April 27. Painted the bath red, and was delighted with the result. Sorry to say Carrie was not, in fact we had a few words about it. She said I ought to have consulted her, and she had never heard of such a thing as a bath being painted red. I replied: 'It's merely a matter of taste.'

Fortunately, further argument on the subject was stopped by a voice saying, 'May I come in?' It was only Cummings, who said, 'Your maid opened the door, and asked me to excuse her showing me in, as she was wringing out some socks.' I was delighted to see him, and suggested we should have a game of whist with a dummy, and by way of merriment said: 'You can be the dummy.' Cummings (I thought rather ill-naturedly) replied: 'Funny as usual.' He said he couldn't stop, he only called to leave me the *Bicycle News*, as he had done with it.

Another ring at the bell; it was Gowing, who said he 'must apologise for coming so often, and that one of these days we must come round to *him*.' I said: 'A very extraordinary thing has struck me.' 'Something funny, as usual,' said Cummings. 'Yes,' I replied; 'I think even you will say so this time. It's concerning you both; for doesn't it seem odd that Gowing's always coming and Cummings' always going?' Carrie, who had evidently quite forgotten about the bath, went into fits of laughter, and as for myself, I fairly doubled up in my chair, till it cracked beneath me. I think this was one of the best jokes I have ever made.

Then imagine my astonishment on perceiving both Cummings and Gowing perfectly silent, and without a smile on their faces. After rather an unpleasant pause, Cummings, who had opened a cigar-case, closed it up again and said: 'Yes – I think, after that, I *shall* be going, and I am sorry I fail to see the fun of your jokes.' Gowing said he didn't mind a joke when it wasn't rude, but a pun on a name, to his thinking, was certainly a little wanting in good taste. Cummings followed it up by saying, if it had been said by anyone else but myself, he shouldn't have entered the house again. This rather unpleasantly terminated what might have been a cheerful evening.

George and Weedon Grossmith,
The Diary of a Nobody

If you are looking for a good reason to indulge in a plate of oysters:

'You needn't tell me that a man who doesn't love oysters and asparagus and good wines has got a soul, or a stomach either. He's simply got the instinct for being unhappy highly developed.'

Clovis relapsed for a few golden moments into tender intimacies with a succession of rapidly disappearing oysters.

'I think oysters are more beautiful than any religion,' he resumed presently. 'They not only forgive our unkindness to them; they justify it, they incite us to go on being perfectly horrid to them. Once they arrive at the supper-table they seem to enter thoroughly into the spirit of the thing. There's nothing in Christianity or Buddhism that quite matches the sympathetic unselfishness of an oyster.'

Saki, *The Chronicles of Clovis*

If you need a little help choosing your desert-island luxury:

'Three years!' I cried. 'Were you shipwrecked?'

'Nay, mate,' said he; 'marooned.'

I had heard the word, and I knew it stood for a horrible kind of punishment common enough among the buccaneers, in which the offender is put ashore with a little powder and shot and left behind on some desolate and distant island.

'Marooned three years agone,' he continued, 'and lived on goats since then, and berries, and oysters. Wherever a man is, says I, a man can do for himself. But, mate, my heart is sore for Christian diet. You mightn't happen to have a piece of cheese about you, now? No? Well, many's the long night I've dreamed of cheese — toasted, mostly — and woke up again, and here I were.'

'If ever I can get aboard again,' said I, 'you shall have cheese by the stone.'

Robert Louis Stevenson, *Treasure Island*

If you find an unattended piece of cake and think it couldn't do any harm to eat it:

Soon her eye fell on a little glass box that was lying under the table: she opened it, and found in it a very small cake, on which the words 'EAT ME' were beautifully marked in currants. 'Well, I'll eat it,' said Alice, 'and if it makes me grow larger, I can reach the key; and if it makes me grow smaller, I can creep under the door; so either way I'll get into the garden, and I don't care which happens!'

She ate a little bit, and said anxiously to herself, 'Which way? Which way?', holding her hand on the top of her head to feel which way it was growing, and she was quite surprised to find that she remained the same size: to be sure, this generally happens when one eats cake, but Alice had got so much into the way of expecting nothing but out-of-the-way things to happen, that it seemed quite dull and stupid for life to go on in the common way.

So she set to work, and very soon finished off the cake.

'Curiouser and curiouser!' cried Alice (she was so much surprised, that for the moment she quite forgot how to speak good English); 'now I'm opening out like the largest telescope that ever was! Good-bye, feet!' (for when she looked down at her feet, they seemed to be almost out of sight, they were getting so far off). 'Oh, my poor little feet, I wonder who will put on your shoes and stockings for you now, dears? I'm sure I shan't be able! I shall be a great deal too far off to trouble myself about you: you must manage the best way you can; – but I must be kind to them,' thought Alice, 'or perhaps they won't walk the way I want to go! Let me see: I'll give them a new pair of boots every Christmas.'

Lewis Carroll, *Alice's Adventures in Wonderland*

If you are inclined to enjoy a long and alcoholic 'working lunch':

Sobriety. Use no description of intoxicating drinks. – As no man can succeed in business unless he has a *brain* to enable him to lay his plans, and *reason* to guide him in their execution, so, no matter how bountifully a man may be blessed with intelligence, if his brain is muddled, and his judgment warped by intoxicating drinks, it is impossible for him to carry on business successfully. How many good opportunities have passed never to return, while a man was sipping a 'social glass' with a friend! How many a foolish bargain has been made under the influence of the wine-cup, which temporarily makes his victim so *rich*! How many important chances have been put off until to-morrow, and thence for ever, because indulgence has thrown the system into a state of lassitude, neutralising the energies so essential to success in business.

Cecil B. Hartley, *The Gentlemen's Book of Etiquette and Manual of Politeness*

If you have the skill to commit a crime, but you're not sure you have strength of character to follow it through:

The officers were satisfied. My manner had convinced them. I was singularly at ease. They sat, and while I answered cheerily, they chatted of familiar things. But, ere long, I felt myself getting pale and wished them gone. My head ached, and I fancied a ringing in my ears: but still they sat and still chatted. The ringing became more distinct: – It continued and became more distinct: I talked more freely to get rid of the feeling: but it continued and gained definiteness – until, at length, I found that the noise was not within my ears.

No doubt I now grew very pale; – but I talked more fluently, and with a heightened voice. Yet the sound increased – and what could I do? It was a low, dull, quick sound – much such a sound as a watch makes when enveloped in cotton. I gasped for breath – and yet the officers heard it not. I talked more quickly – more vehemently; but the noise steadily increased.

I arose and argued about trifles, in a high key and with violent gesticulations; but the noise steadily increased. Why would they not be gone? I paced the floor to and fro with heavy strides, as if excited to fury by the observations of the men – but the noise steadily increased. Oh God! what could I do? I foamed – I raved – I swore! I swung the chair upon which I had been sitting, and grated it upon the boards, but the noise arose over all and continually increased. It grew louder – louder – louder! And still the men chatted pleasantly, and smiled. Was it possible they heard not? Almighty God! – no, no! They heard! – they suspected! – they knew! – they were making a mockery of my horror! – this I thought, and this I think. But anything was better than this agony! Anything was more tolerable than this derision! I could bear those hypocritical smiles no longer! I felt that I must scream or die! and now – again! – hark! louder! louder! louder! louder!

'Villains!' I shrieked, 'dissemble no more! I admit the deed! – tear up the planks! here, here! – It is the beating of his hideous heart!'

Edgar Allan Poe, 'The Tell-Tale Heart'

FAMILY

If you are short of space and need to improvise a bed for a visiting relative:

After looking around attentively in the room, she asked, 'Where am I going to sleep, grandfather?'

'Wherever you want to,' he replied. That suited Heidi exactly. She peeped into all the corners of the room and looked at every little nook to find a cosy place to sleep. Beside the old man's bed she saw a ladder. Climbing up, she arrived at a hayloft, which was filled with fresh and fragrant hay. Through a tiny round window she could look far down into the valley.

'I want to sleep up here,' Heidi called down. 'Oh, it is lovely here. Please come up, grandfather, and see it for yourself.'

'I know it,' sounded from below.

'I am making the bed now,' the little girl called out again, while she ran busily to and fro. 'Oh, do come up and bring a sheet, grandfather, for every bed must have a sheet.'

'Is that so?' said the old man. After a while he opened the cupboard and rummaged around in it. At last he pulled out a long coarse cloth from under the shirts. It somewhat resembled a sheet, and with this he climbed up to the loft. Here a neat little bed was already prepared. On top the hay was heaped up high so that the head of the occupant would lie exactly opposite the window.

Johanna Spyri, *Heidi*

If you feel embarrassed about singing to your baby:

I think my life began with waking up and loving my mother's face: it was so near to me, and her arms were round me, and she sang to me. One hymn she sang so often, so often: and then she taught me to sing it with her: it was the first I ever sang. They were always Hebrew hymns she sang; and because I never knew the meaning of the words they seemed full of nothing but our love and happiness. When I lay in my little bed and it was all white above me, she used to bend over me, between me and the white, and sing in a sweet, low voice. I can dream myself back into that time when I am awake, and it often comes back to me in my sleep – my hand is very little, I put it up to her face and she kisses it.

George Eliot, *Daniel Deronda*

If you need any help persuading your children to eat their greens:

CABBAGE, n. A familiar kitchen-garden vegetable about as large and wise as a man's head.

The cabbage is so called from Cabagius, a prince who on ascending the throne issued a decree appointing a High Council of Empire consisting of the members of his predecessor's Ministry and the cabbages in the royal garden. When any of his Majesty's measures of state policy miscarried conspicuously it was gravely announced that several members of the High Council had been beheaded, and his murmuring subjects were appeased.

Ambrose Bierce, *The Devil's Dictionary*

If you wonder whether there's a better alternative to having the whole family staring at the TV during mealtimes:

Both dinner and supper are begun with some lecture of morality that is read to them; but it is so short that it is not tedious nor uneasy to them to hear it. From hence the old men take occasion to entertain those about them with some useful and pleasant enlargements; but they do not engross the whole discourse so to themselves during their meals that the younger may not put in for a share; on the contrary, they engage them to talk, that so they may, in that free way of conversation, find out the force of every one's spirit and observe his temper. They despatch their dinners quickly, but sit long at supper, because they go to work after the one, and are to sleep after the other, during which they think the stomach carries on the concoction more vigorously. They never sup without music, and there is always fruit served up after meat; while they are at table some burn perfumes and sprinkle about fragrant ointments and sweet waters

– in short, they want nothing that may cheer up their spirits; they give themselves a large allowance that way, and indulge themselves in all such pleasures as are attended with no inconvenience.

Thomas More, *Utopia*

If other members of the family criticise you for being too particular about having your bed exactly how you like it:

One evening a fearful tempest arose, it thundered and lightened, and the rain poured down from the sky in torrents: besides, it was as dark as pitch. All at once there was heard a violent knocking at the door, and the old King, the Prince's father, went out himself to open it.

It was a Princess who was standing outside the door. What with the rain and the wind, she was in a sad condition; the water trickled down from her hair, and her clothes clung to her body. She said she was a real Princess.

'Ah! we shall soon see that!' thought the old Queen-mother; however, she said not a word of what she was going to do; but went quietly into the bedroom, took all the bed-clothes off the bed, and put three little peas on the bedstead. She then laid twenty mattresses one upon another over the three peas, and put twenty feather beds over the mattresses.

Upon this bed the Princess was to pass the night.

The next morning she was asked how she had slept. 'Oh, very badly indeed!' she replied. 'I have scarcely closed my eyes the whole night through. I do not know what was in my bed, but I had something hard under me, and am all over black and blue. It has hurt me so much!'

Now it was plain that the lady must be a real Princess, since she had been able to feel the three little peas through the twenty mattresses and twenty feather beds. None but a real Princess could have had such a delicate sense of feeling.

Hans Christian Andersen, *Fairy Tales Told for Children. First Collection*

If you need to give some fatherly advice before a long journey:

Give thy thoughts no tongue,
Nor any unproportion'd thought his act.
Be thou familiar, but by no means vulgar.
Those friends thou hast, and their adoption tried,
Grapple them unto thy soul with hoops of steel;
But do not dull thy palm with entertainment
Of each new-hatch'd, unfledg'd comrade. Beware
Of entrance to a quarrel; but, being in,
Bear't that the opposed may beware of thee.
Give every man thine ear, but few thy voice:
Take each man's censure, but reserve thy judgment.
Costly thy habit as thy purse can buy,
But not express'd in fancy; rich, not gaudy:
For the apparel oft proclaims the man;
And they in France of the best rank and station
Are most select and generous chief in that.
Neither a borrower nor a lender be:
For loan oft loses both itself and friend;
And borrowing dulls the edge of husbandry.
This above all, – to thine own self be true;

And it must follow, as the night the day,
Thou canst not then be false to any man.
Farewell: my blessing season this in thee!

William Shakespeare, *Hamlet*

If you need to find a polite way to bring a family member's musical recital to a close:

Elizabeth now began to revive. But not long was the interval of tranquillity; for, when supper was over, singing was talked of, and she had the mortification of seeing Mary, after very little entreaty, preparing to oblige the company. By many significant looks and silent entreaties, did she endeavour to prevent such a proof of complaisance, but in vain; Mary would not understand them; such an opportunity of exhibiting was delightful to her, and she began her song. Elizabeth's eyes were fixed on her with most painful sensations, and she watched her progress through the several stanzas with an impatience which was very ill rewarded at their close; for Mary, on receiving, amongst the thanks of the table, the hint of a hope that she might be prevailed on to favour them again, after the pause of half a minute began another. Mary's powers were by no means fitted for such a display; her voice was weak, and her manner affected. Elizabeth was in agonies. She looked at Jane, to see how she bore it; but Jane was very composedly talking to Bingley. She looked at his two sisters, and saw them making signs of derision at each other, and at Darcy, who continued, however, imperturbably grave. She looked at her father to entreat his interference, lest Mary should be singing all night. He took the hint, and when Mary had finished her second song, said aloud, 'That will do extremely well, child. You have delighted us long enough. Let the other young ladies have time to exhibit.'

Jane Austen, *Pride and Prejudice*

If you are wondering why different generations sometimes find it hard to understand each other:

Every age of man has a certain philosophy answering to it. The child comes out as a realist: he finds himself as convinced that pears and apples exist as that he himself exists. The youth in a storm of inner passion is forced to turn his gaze within, and feel in advance what he is going to be: he is changed into an idealist. But the man has every reason to become a sceptic: he does well to doubt whether the means he has chosen to his end are the right ones. Before and during action he has every reason for keeping his understanding mobile, that he may not afterwards have to grieve over a false choice. Yet when he grows old he will always confess himself a mystic: he sees that so much seems to depend on chance; that folly succeeds and wisdom fails; that good and evil fortune are brought unexpectedly to the same level; so it is and so it has been, and old age acquiesces in that which is and was and will be.

Johann Wolfgang von Goethe, *Maxims and Reflections*

64

CHILDHOOD AND GROWING UP

If adults tell you that your behaviour isn't mature enough:

Jo immediately sat up, put her hands in her pockets, and began to whistle.

'Don't, Jo. It's so boyish!'

'That's why I do it.'

'I detest rude, unladylike girls!'

'I hate affected, niminy-piminy chits!'

'Birds in their little nests agree,' sang Beth, the peacemaker, with such a funny face that both sharp voices softened to a laugh, and the 'pecking' ended for that time.

'Really, girls, you are both to be blamed,' said Meg, beginning to lecture in her elder-sisterly fashion. 'You are old enough to leave off boyish tricks, and to behave better, Josephine. It didn't matter so much when you were a little girl, but now you are so tall, and turn up your hair, you should remember that you are a young lady.'

'I'm not! And if turning up my hair makes me one, I'll wear it in two tails till I'm twenty,' cried Jo, pulling off her net, and shaking down a chestnut mane. 'I hate to think I've got to grow up, and be Miss March, and wear long gowns, and look as prim as a China Aster! It's bad enough to be a girl, anyway, when I like boy's games and work and manners! I can't get over my disappointment in not being a boy. And it's worse than ever now, for I'm dying to go and fight with Papa. And I can only stay home and knit, like a poky old woman!'

And Jo shook the blue army sock till the needles rattled like castanets, and her ball bounded across the room.

Louisa May Alcott, *Little Women*

If you want to understand why your teeth fall out when you're a child:

'Will you give me a lump of sugar?' he asked in a sharp, hard little voice – a voice immature and yet, somehow, not young.

Winterbourne glanced at the small table near him, on which his coffee service rested, and saw that several morsels of sugar remained. 'Yes, you may take one,' he answered; 'but I don't think sugar is good for little boys.'

This little boy stepped forward and carefully selected three of the coveted fragments, two of which he buried in the pocket of his knickerbockers, depositing the other as promptly in another place. He poked his alpenstock, lance-fashion, into Winterbourne's bench and tried to crack the lump of sugar with his teeth.

'Oh, blazes; it's har-r-d!' he exclaimed, pronouncing the adjective in a peculiar manner.

Winterbourne had immediately perceived that he might have the honour of claiming him as a fellow countryman. 'Take care you don't hurt your teeth,' he said, paternally.

'I haven't got any teeth to hurt. They have all come out. I have only got seven teeth. My mother counted them last night, and one came out right afterward. She said she'd slap me if any more came out. I can't help it. It's this old Europe. It's the climate that makes them come out. In America they didn't come out. It's these hotels.'

Henry James, *Daisy Miller*

If you need to pass yourself off as a girl, and not the tough country boy you really are:

'What's your real name, now?'

'George Peters, mum.'

'Well, try to remember it, George. Don't forget and tell me it's Elexander before you go, and then get out by saying it's George Elexander when I catch you. And don't go about women in that old calico. You do a girl tolerable poor, but you might fool men, maybe. Bless you, child, when you set out to thread a needle don't hold the thread still and fetch the needle up to it; hold the needle still and poke the thread at it; that's the way a woman most always does, but a man always does t'other way. And when you throw at a rat or anything, hitch yourself up a tiptoe and fetch your hand up over your head as awkward as you can, and miss your rat about six or seven foot. Throw stiff-armed from the shoulder, like there was a pivot there for it to turn on, like a girl; not from the wrist and elbow, with your arm out to one side, like a boy. And, mind you, when a girl tries to catch anything in her lap she throws her knees apart; she don't clap them together, the way you did when you catched the lump of lead. Why, I spotted you for a boy when you was threading the needle; and I contrived the other things just to make certain. Now trot along to your uncle, Sarah Mary Williams George Elexander Peters, and if you get into trouble you send word to Mrs Judith Loftus, which is me, and I'll do what I can to get you out of it. Keep the river road all the way, and next time you tramp take shoes and socks with you. The river road's a rocky one, and your feet'll be in a condition when you get to Goshen, I reckon.'

Mark Twain, *The Adventures of Huckleberry Finn*

If you feel that nobody can understand the struggles of being 'the middle child':

Then came Elsie, a thin, brown child of eight, with beautiful dark eyes, and crisp, short curls covering the whole of her small head. Poor little Elsie was the 'odd one' among the Carrs. She didn't seem to belong exactly to either the older or the younger children. The great desire and ambition of her heart was to be allowed to go about with Katy and Clover and Cecy Hall, and to know their secrets, and be permitted to put notes into the little post-offices they were forever establishing in all sorts of hidden places. But they didn't want Elsie, and used to tell her to 'run away and play with the children', which hurt her feelings very much. When she wouldn't run away, I am sorry to say they ran away from her, which, as their legs were longest, it was easy to do. Poor Elsie, left behind, would cry bitter tears, and, as she was too proud to play much with Dorry and John, her principal comfort was tracking the older ones about and discovering their mysteries, especially the post-offices, which were her greatest grievance. Her eyes were bright and quick as a bird's. She would peep and peer, and follow and watch, till at last, in some odd, unlikely place, the crotch of a tree, the middle of the asparagus bed, or, perhaps, on the very top step of the scuttle ladder, she spied the little paper box, with its load of notes, all ending with: 'Be sure and not let Elsie know.' Then she would seize the box, and, marching up to wherever the others were, she would throw it down, saying, defiantly: 'There's your old post-office!' but feeling all the time just like crying. Poor little Elsie! In almost every big family, there is one of these unmated, left-out children. Katy, who had the finest plans in the world for being 'heroic', and of use, never saw, as she drifted on her heedless way, that here, in this lonely little sister, was the very chance she wanted for being a comfort to somebody who needed comfort very much. She never saw it, and Elsie's heavy heart went uncheered.

Susan Coolidge, *What Katy Did*

If you want to make your last day at school a memorable one:

'Stop!' cried Miss Jemima, rushing to the gate with a parcel.

'It's some sandwiches, my dear,' said she to Amelia. 'You may be hungry, you know; and Becky, Becky Sharp, here's a book for you that my sister – that is, I – Johnson's Dixonary, you know; you mustn't leave us without that. Good-by. Drive on, coachman. God bless you!'

And the kind creature retreated into the garden, overcome with emotion.

But, lo! and just as the coach drove off, Miss Sharp put her pale face out of the window and actually flung the book back into the garden.

This almost caused Jemima to faint with terror. 'Well, I never' – said she – 'what an audacious' – Emotion prevented her from completing either sentence. The carriage rolled away; the great gates were closed; the bell rang for the dancing lesson. The world is before the two young ladies; and so, farewell to Chiswick Mall.

William Makepeace Thackeray, *Vanity Fair*

If you ever wonder why your mother always tells you so very much detail in her letters and phone calls:

Meanwhile, poor Betty Flanders's letter, having caught the second post, lay on the hall table – poor Betty Flanders writing her son's name, Jacob Alan Flanders, Esq., as mothers do, and the ink pale, profuse, suggesting how mothers down at Scarborough scribble over the fire with their feet on the fender, when tea's cleared away, and can never, never say, whatever it may be – probably this – Don't go with bad women, do be a good boy; wear your thick shirts; and come back, come back, come back to me.

But she said nothing of the kind. 'Do you remember old Miss Wargrave, who used to be so kind when you had the whooping-cough?' she wrote; 'she's dead at last, poor thing. They would like it if you wrote. Ellen came over and we spent a nice day shopping. Old Mouse gets very stiff, and we have to walk him up the smallest hill. Rebecca, at last, after I don't know how long, went into Mr Adamson's. Three teeth, he says, must come out. Such mild weather for the time of year, the little buds actually on the pear trees. And Mrs Jarvis tells me —'

Virginia Woolf, *Jacob's Room*

If you think being a parent must be a pretty easy job:

'Imagine what it must be to have an unborn quartered upon you, who is of an entirely different temperament and disposition to your own; nay, half-a-dozen such, who will not love you though you have stinted yourself in a thousand ways to provide for their comfort and well-being, – who will forget all your self-sacrifice, and of whom you may never be sure that they are not bearing a grudge against you for errors of judgement into which you may have fallen, though you had hoped that such had been long since atoned for. Ingratitude such as this is not uncommon, yet fancy what it must be to bear! It is hard upon the duckling to have been hatched by a hen, but is it not also hard upon the hen to have hatched the duckling?'

Samuel Butler, *Erewhon*

If people tell you the subjects you want to study are not important or serious enough:

The intellect will always profit by the acquisition of any knowledge whatsoever, for thus what is useless will be expelled from it, and what is fruitful will remain. It is impossible either to hate or to love a thing without first acquiring knowledge of it.

Men of worth naturally desire knowledge.

Leonardo da Vinci, *Thoughts on Art and Life*

LOVE AND ROMANCE

If you want to know what men and women really want from each other:

What is it men in women do require?
The lineaments of gratified desire.
What is it women do in men require?
The lineaments of gratified desire.

William Blake, from 'Several Questions Answered'

If you need some ideas for the perfect date:

Spending nights playing with dice. Going out on moonlight nights. Keeping the festive day in honour of spring. Plucking the sprouts and fruits of the mangoe trees. Eating the fibres of lotuses. Eating the tender ears of corn. Picnicing in the forests when the trees get their new foliage. The Udakakashvedika or sporting in the water. Decorating each other with the flowers of some trees. Pelting each other with the flowers of the Kadamba tree, and many other sports which may either be known to the whole country, or may be peculiar to particular parts of it. These and similar other amusements should always be carried on by citizens.

The Kama Sutra of Vātsyāyana

If you long for a foolproof way to find out who your true love will be:

The snail charm, described by Gay in the 'Shepherd's Week', though probably of English extraction, is even yet very general in Ireland, but is chiefly performed by the girls. The little animal pressed into the service on this occasion is not the box-snail (or shellemidah), but what is commonly called the Drutheen, or slug, and should be discovered accidentally, not sought for; when found, it is either placed between two pewter plates, or upon a table previously sprinkled with ashes or flour, and covered with a mias, or wooden bowl; and in the morning the anxious maid seeks to discover in the slimy track left by the snail's nocturnal peregrinations, the initial of her secret lover's name: –

'Slow crawl'd the snail, and if I right can spell,
In the soft ashes marked a curious L;
Oh, may the wondrous omen lucky prove!
For L is found in Lubberkin and Love.'

William Wilde, *Ireland: Her Wit, Peculiarities and Popular Superstitions*

If you want to persuade your friends that you are perfectly happy being single*:

LEONATO: By my troth, niece, thou wilt never get thee a husband if thou be so shrewd of thy tongue.

ANTONIO: In faith, she's too curst.

BEATRICE: Too curst is more than curst. I shall lessen God's sending that way, for it is said, 'God sends a curst cow short horns,' but to a cow too curst he sends none.

LEONATO: So, by being too curst, God will send you no horns.

BEATRICE: Just, if he send me no husband; for the which blessing I am at him upon my knees every morning and evening. Lord, I could not endure a husband with a beard on his face. I had rather lie in the woollen!

LEONATO: You may light on a husband that hath no beard.

BEATRICE: What should I do with him? dress him in my apparel and make him my waiting-gentlewoman?

He that hath a beard is more than a youth, and he that hath no beard is less than a man; and he that is more than a youth is not for me; and he that is less than a man, I am not for him. Therefore I will even take sixpence in earnest of the bear-ward, and lead his apes into hell.

LEONATO: Well then, go you into hell?

BEATRICE: No; but to the gate, and there will the devil meet me, like an old cuckold, with horns on his head, and say 'Get you to heaven, Beatrice, get you to heaven. Here's no place for you maids.' So deliver I up my apes, and away to Saint Peter for the heavens. He shows me where the bachelors sit, and there live we as merry as the day is long.

ANTONIO [*to Hero*]: Well, niece, I trust you will be rul'd by your father.

BEATRICE: Yes faith. It is my cousin's duty to make cur'sy and say, 'Father, as it please you.' But yet for all that, cousin, let him be a handsome fellow, or else make another curtsy, and say, 'Father, as it please me.'

LEONATO: Well, niece, I hope to see you one day fitted with a husband.

BEATRICE: Not till God make men of some other metal than earth. Would it not grieve a woman to be overmaster'd with a piece of valiant dust? to make an account of her life to a clod of wayward marl? No, uncle, I'll none. Adam's sons are my brethren, and truly I hold it a sin to match in my kindred.

William Shakespeare, *Much Ado About Nothing*

*Your friends may not believe you

If you are sick and tired of reading dating advice that tells women to be demure and agreeable if they want to win a man:

How grossly do they insult us, who thus advise us only to render ourselves gentle, domestic brutes! For instance, the winning softness, so warmly, and frequently recommended, that governs by obeying. What childish expressions, and how insignificant is the being – can it be an immortal one? who will condescend to govern by such sinister methods!

Mary Wollstonecraft, *A Vindication of the Rights of Woman*

If you have fallen in love with somebody's looks, but you know your characters are miles apart:

Thus, whether it be Wit or Beauty that a Man's in Love with, there's no great hopes of a lasting Happiness; Beauty with all the helps of Art is of no very lasting date, the more it is help'd the sooner it decays, and he who only or chiefly chose for Beauty, will in a little time find the same reason for another choice. Nor is that sort of Wit which he prefers of a more sure tenure, or allowing it to last, it will not always please. For that which has not a real excellency and value in it self, entertains no longer than that giddy Humour which recommended it to us holds; and when we can like on no just, or on very little Ground, 'tis certain a dislike will arise, as lightly and as unaccountably. And it is not improbable that such a Husband may in a little time by ill usage provoke such a Wife to exercise her Wit, that is, her Spleen on him, and then it is not hard to guess how very agreeable it will be to him.

Mary Astell, *Some Reflections Upon Marriage*

If you fear you're too old to find love again:

And this girl, who united all these qualities, loved him. He was a modest man, but he could not help seeing it. And he loved her. There was one consideration against it – his age. But he came of a long-lived family, he had not a single grey hair, no one would have taken him for forty, and he remembered Varenka's saying that it was only in Russia that men of fifty thought themselves old, and that in France a man of fifty considers himself *dans la force de l'âge*, while a man of forty is *un jeune homme*. But what did the mere reckoning of years matter when he felt as young in heart as he had been twenty years ago?

Leo Tolstoy, *Anna Karenina*

If you suspect you might be in love, but you're unsure because it wasn't a whirlwind romance:

For a moment Anne's heart fluttered queerly and for the first time her eyes faltered under Gilbert's gaze and a rosy flush stained the paleness of her face. It was as if a veil that had hung before her inner consciousness had been lifted, giving to her view a revelation of unsuspected feelings and realities. Perhaps, after all, romance did not come into one's life with pomp and blare, like a gay knight riding down; perhaps it crept to one's side like an old friend through quiet ways; perhaps it revealed itself in seeming prose, until some sudden shaft of illumination flung athwart its pages betrayed the rhythm and the music, perhaps... perhaps... love unfolded naturally out of a beautiful friendship, as a golden-hearted rose slipping from its green sheath.

L. M. Montgomery, *Anne of Avonlea*

If your lover has proposed to you, and you don't know how to answer:

'What shall I do? What would you advise me to do? Pray, dear Miss Woodhouse, tell me what I ought to do.'

'I shall not give you any advice, Harriet. I will have nothing to do with it. This is a point which you must settle with your feelings.'

'I had no notion that he liked me so very much,' said Harriet, contemplating the letter. For a little while Emma persevered in her silence; but beginning to apprehend the bewitching flattery of that letter might be too powerful, she thought it best to say,

'I lay it down as a general rule, Harriet, that if a woman doubts as to whether she should accept a man or not, she certainly ought to refuse him. If she can hesitate as to "Yes", she ought to say "No" directly. It is not a state to be safely entered into with doubtful feelings, with half a heart. I thought it my duty as a friend, and older than yourself, to say thus much to you. But do not imagine that I want to influence you.'

Jane Austen, *Emma*

If you thought housework and erotic pleasure could never be combined:

Then said Giannello, 'The vat appeareth to me sound enough; but meseemeth you have kept dregs or the like therein, for it is all overcrusted with I know not what that is so hard and dry that I cannot remove aught thereof with my nails; wherefore I will not take it, except I first see it clean.' 'Nay,' answered Peronella, 'the bargain shall not fall through for that; my husband will clean it all out.' 'Ay will I,' rejoined the latter, and laying down his tools, put off his coat; then, calling for a light and a scraper, he entered the vat and fell to scraping. Peronella, as if she had a mind to see what he did, thrust her head and one of her arms, shoulder and all, in at the mouth of the vat, which was not overbig, and fell to saying, 'Scrape here' and 'There' and 'There also' and 'See, here is a little left'.

Whilst she was thus engaged in directing her husband and showing him where to scrape, Giannello, who had scarce yet that morning done his full desire, when they were interrupted by the mason's coming, seeing that he could not as he would, bethought himself to accomplish it as he might; wherefore, boarding her, as she held the mouth of the vat all closed up, on such wise as in the ample plains the unbridled stallions, afire with love, assail the mares of Parthia, he satisfied his juvenile ardour, the which enterprise was brought to perfection well nigh at the same moment as the scraping of the vat; whereupon he dismounted and Peronella withdrawing her head from the mouth of the vat, the husband came forth thereof.

Giovanni Boccaccio, *The Decameron*

If you wonder why your feelings of love refuse to be tamed:

Love is no hot-house flower, but a wild plant, born of a wet night, born of an hour of sunshine; sprung from wild seed, blown along the road by a wild wind. A wild plant that, when it blooms by chance within the hedge of our gardens, we call a flower; and when it blooms outside we call a weed; but, flower or weed, whose scent and colour are always, wild!

John Galsworthy, *The Man of Property*

WORKING LIFE

If you wish to avoid work, in the most frustrating way possible:

In this very attitude did I sit when I called to him, rapidly stating what it was I wanted him to do – namely, to examine a small paper with me. Imagine my surprise, nay, my consternation, when without moving from his privacy, Bartleby in a singularly mild, firm voice, replied, 'I would prefer not to.'

I sat awhile in perfect silence, rallying my stunned faculties. Immediately it occurred to me that my ears had deceived me, or Bartleby had entirely misunderstood my meaning. I repeated my request in the clearest tone I could assume. But in quite as clear a one came the previous reply, 'I would prefer not to.'

'Prefer not to,' echoed I, rising in high excitement, and crossing the room with a stride. 'What do you mean? Are you moon-struck? I want you to help me compare this sheet here – take it,' and I thrust it towards him.

'I would prefer not to,' said he.

Herman Melville, *Bartleby, the Scrivener*

If you are tired of typing all day and feel nostalgic for the days of handwriting:

My hand is weary with writing,
My sharp quill is not steady,
My slender-beaked pen juts forth
A black draught of shining dark-blue ink.

A stream of the wisdom of blessed God
Springs from my fair-brown shapely hand:
On the page it squirts its draught
Of ink of the green-skinned holly.

My little dripping pen travels
Across the plain of shining books,
Without ceasing for the wealth of the great –
Whence my hand is weary with writing.

Columbanus, 'Columcille the Scribe'

If you need some encouragement to help you break through the glass ceiling at work:

I know I have the body of a weak, feeble woman; but I have the heart and stomach of a king, and of a king of England too, and think foul scorn that Parma or Spain, or any prince of Europe, should dare to invade the borders of my realm; to which rather than any dishonour shall grow by me, I myself will take up arms, I myself will be your general, judge, and rewarder of every one of your virtues in the field.

Queen Elizabeth I, speech to the troops at Tilbury

If you are looking for advice on recruitment techniques:

One day he saw it advertised in a newspaper that the secretary of a hospital in the north of London was in need of a clerk; application was to be made by letter. He wrote, and two days later, to his astonishment, received a reply asking him to wait upon the secretary at a certain hour. In a fever of agitation he kept the appointment, and found that his business was with a young man in the very highest spirits, who walked up and down a little office (the hospital was of the 'special' order, a house of no great size), and treated the matter in hand as an excellent joke.

'I thought, you know, of engaging someone much younger – quite a lad, in fact. But look there! Those are the replies to my advertisement.'

He pointed to a heap of five or six hundred letters, and laughed consumedly.

'Impossible to read them all, you know. It seemed to me that the fairest thing would be to shake them together, stick my hand in, and take out one by chance. If it didn't seem very promising, I would try a second time. But the first letter was yours, and I thought the fair thing to do was at all events to see you, you know. The fact is, I am only able to offer a pound a week.'

'I shall be very glad indeed to take that,' said Reardon, who was bathed in perspiration.

'Then what about references, and so on?' proceeded the young man, chuckling and rubbing his hands together.

The applicant was engaged.

George Gissing, *New Grub Street*

If you tend to surround yourself at work only with people who agree with your every word:

I do not wish to leave out an important branch of this subject, for it is a danger from which princes are with difficulty preserved, unless they are very careful and discriminating. It is that of flatterers, of whom courts are full, because men are so self-complacent in their own affairs, and in a way so deceived in them, that they are preserved with difficulty from this pest, and if they wish to defend themselves they run the danger of falling into contempt. Because there is no other way of guarding oneself from flatterers except letting men understand that to tell you the truth does not offend you; but when every one may tell you the truth, respect for you abates.

Therefore a wise prince ought to hold a third course by choosing the wise men in his state, and giving to them only the liberty of speaking the truth to him, and then only of those things of which he inquires, and of none others; but he ought to question them upon everything, and listen to their opinions, and afterwards form his own conclusions. With these councillors, separately and collectively, he ought to carry himself in such a way that each of them should know that, the more freely he shall speak, the more he shall be preferred; outside of these, he should listen to no one, pursue the thing resolved on, and be steadfast in his resolutions. He who does otherwise is either overthrown by flatterers, or is so often changed by varying opinions that he falls into contempt.

Niccolò Machiavelli, *The Prince*

If you suddenly realise you've taken too long over your lunch break and need to make yourself look busy:

At this moment a footstep was heard in the passage leading to the kitchen. Old Misery! or perhaps the bloke himself! Cross hurriedly pulled out his watch.

'Jesus Christ!' he gasped. 'It's four minutes past one!'

Linden frantically seized hold of a pair of steps and began wandering about the room with them.

Sawkins scrambled hastily to his feet and, snatching a piece of sandpaper from the pocket of his apron, began furiously rubbing down the scullery door.

Easton threw down the copy of the *Obscurer* and scrambled hastily to his feet.

The boy crammed the *Chronicles of Crime* into his trousers pocket.

Cross rushed over to the bucket and began stirring up the stale whitewash it contained, and the stench which it gave forth was simply appalling.

Consternation reigned.

They looked like a gang of malefactors suddenly interrupted in the commission of a crime.

The door opened. It was only Bundy returning from his mission to the Bookie.

Robert Tressell, *The Ragged Trousered Philanthropists*

If you are looking for a good technique to get others to do your work for you:

'Hello, old chap, you got to work, hey?'

Tom wheeled suddenly and said:

'Why, it's you, Ben! I warn't noticing.'

'Say – I'm going in a-swimming, I am. Don't you wish you could? But of course you'd druther work – wouldn't you? Course you would!' Tom contemplated the boy a bit, and said:

'What do you call work?'

'Why, ain't that work?'

Tom resumed his whitewashing, and answered carelessly:

'Well, maybe it is, and maybe it ain't. All I know, is, it suits Tom Sawyer.'

'Oh come, now, you don't mean to let on that you like it?'

The brush continued to move.

'Like it? Well, I don't see why I oughtn't to like it. Does a boy get a chance to whitewash a fence every day?'

That put the thing in a new light. Ben stopped nibbling his apple. Tom swept his brush daintily back and forth – stepped back to note the effect – added a touch here and there – criticised the effect again – Ben watching every move and getting more and more interested, more and more absorbed. Presently he said:

'Say, Tom, let me whitewash a little.'

Mark Twain, *The Adventures of Tom Sawyer*

If you need to find a cheerful perspective on the fact that you have to work for a living:

'There's nothing but what's bearable as long as a man can work,' he said to himself; 'the natur o' things doesn't change, though it seems as if one's own life was nothing but change. The square o' four is sixteen, and you must lengthen your lever in proportion to your weight, is as true when a man's miserable as when he's happy; and the best o' working is, it gives you a grip hold o' things outside your own lot.'

George Eliot, *Adam Bede*

If you fear that you are putting too much of your precious time and energy into your work:

The different accidents of life are not so changeable as the feelings of human nature. I had worked hard for nearly two years, for the sole purpose of infusing life into an inanimate body. For this I had deprived myself of rest and health. I had desired it with an ardour that far exceeded moderation; but now that I had finished, the beauty of the dream vanished, and breathless horror and disgust filled my heart.

Mary Shelley, *Frankenstein*

If you think a teacher's life has nothing to offer you but endless marking:

The schoolmaster is generally a man of some importance in the female circle of a rural neighbourhood; being considered a kind of idle, gentlemanlike personage, of vastly superior taste and accomplishments to the rough country swains, and, indeed, inferior in learning only to the parson. His appearance, therefore, is apt to occasion some little stir at the tea-table of a farmhouse, and the addition of a supernumerary dish of cakes or sweetmeats, or, peradventure, the parade of a silver teapot. Our man of letters, therefore, was peculiarly happy in the smiles of all the country damsels. How he would figure among them in the churchyard, between services on Sundays; gathering grapes for them from the wild vines that overran the surrounding trees; reciting for their amusement all the epitaphs on the tombstones; or sauntering, with a whole bevy of them, along the banks of the adjacent millpond; while the more bashful country bumpkins hung sheepishly back, envying his superior elegance and address.

Washington Irving, 'The Legend of Sleepy Hollow'

If you are wondering what benefits a sailor's life might offer you:

I always go to sea as a sailor, because they make a point of paying me for my trouble, whereas they never pay passengers a single penny that I ever heard of. On the contrary, passengers themselves must pay. And there is all the difference in the world between paying and being paid. The act of paying is perhaps the most uncomfortable infliction that the two orchard thieves entailed upon us. But *being paid*, − what will compare with it?

Herman Melville, *Moby-Dick*

If you have ever wondered what it would be like to become an astronomer:

And thus they talked on about Sirius, and then about other stars

> ... in the scrowl
> Of all those beasts, and fish, and fowl,
> With which, like Indian plantations,
> The learned stock the constellations,

till he asked her how many stars she thought were visible to them at that moment.

She looked around over the magnificent stretch of sky that their high position unfolded. 'Oh, thousands, hundreds of thousands,' she said absently.

'No. There are only about three thousand. Now, how many do you think are brought within sight by the help of a powerful telescope?'

'I won't guess.'

'Twenty millions. So that, whatever the stars were made for, they were not made to please our eyes. It is just the same in everything; nothing is made for man.'

'Is it that notion which makes you so sad for your age?' she asked, with almost maternal solicitude. 'I think astronomy is a bad study for you. It makes you feel human insignificance too plainly.'

'Perhaps it does. However,' he added more cheerfully, 'though I feel the study to be one almost tragic in its quality, I hope to be the new Copernicus. What he was to the solar system I aim to be to the systems beyond.'

Thomas Hardy, *Two on a Tower*

LEISURE
TIME

If you are looking for an unusual pet that will be a good friend:

'We have been afield, mother — leaping ditches, scrambling through hedges, running down steep banks, up and away, and hurrying on. The wind has been blowing, and the rushes and young plants bowing and bending to it, lest it should do them harm, the cowards — and Grip — ha ha ha! — brave Grip, who cares for nothing, and when the wind rolls him over in the dust, turns manfully to bite it — Grip, bold Grip, has quarrelled with every little bowing twig — thinking, he told me, that it mocked him — and has worried it like a bulldog. Ha ha ha!'

The raven, in his little basket at his master's back, hearing this frequent mention of his name in a tone of exultation, expressed his sympathy by crowing like a cock, and afterwards running over his various phrases of speech with such rapidity, and in so many varieties of hoarseness, that they sounded like the murmurs of a crowd of people.

'He takes such care of me besides!' said Barnaby. 'Such care, mother! He watches all the time I sleep, and when I shut my eyes and make-believe to slumber, he practises new learning softly; but he keeps his eye on me the while, and if he sees me laugh, though never so little, stops directly. He won't surprise me till he's perfect.'

The raven crowed again in a rapturous manner which plainly said, 'Those are certainly some of my characteristics, and I glory in them.'

Charles Dickens, *Barnaby Rudge*

... and if you need help naming it:

'It's one of her strange ways that she'll never tell the names of these birds if she can help it, though she named 'em all.' This was in a whisper. 'Shall I run 'em over, Flite?' he asked aloud, winking at us and pointing at her as she turned away, affecting to sweep the grate.

'If you like,' she answered hurriedly.

The old man, looking up at the cages after another look at us, went through the list.

'Hope, Joy, Youth, Peace, Rest, Life, Dust, Ashes, Waste, Want, Ruin, Despair, Madness, Death, Cunning, Folly, Words, Wigs, Rags, Sheepskin, Plunder, Precedent, Jargon, Gammon, and Spinach. That's the whole collection,' said the old man, 'all cooped up together, by my noble and learned brother.'

Charles Dickens, *Bleak House*

If you worry that there might be only one 'correct' way to appreciate classical music:

It will be generally admitted that Beethoven's *Fifth Symphony* is the most sublime noise that has ever penetrated into the ear of man. All sorts and conditions are satisfied by it. Whether you are like Mrs Munt, and tap surreptitiously when the tunes come – of course, not so as to disturb the others–; or like Helen, who can see heroes and shipwrecks in the music's flood; or like Margaret, who can only see the music; or like Tibby, who is profoundly versed in counterpoint, and holds the full score open on his knee; or like their cousin, Fräulein Mosebach, who remembers all the time that Beethoven is 'echt Deutsch'; or like Fräulein Mosebach's young man, who can remember nothing but Fräulein Mosebach: in any case, the passion of your life becomes more vivid, and you are bound to admit that such a noise is cheap at two shillings.

E. M. Forster, *Howards End*

If you need to find an excuse for only playing the slow movements of famous pieces to your friends:

When she played the piano as she frequently did, (reserving an hour for practice every day), she cared not in the smallest degree for what anybody who passed down the road outside her house might be thinking of the roulades that poured from her open window: she was simply Emmeline Lucas, absorbed in glorious Bach or dainty Scarletti, or noble Beethoven. The latter perhaps was her favourite composer, and many were the evenings when with lights quenched and only the soft effulgence of the moon pouring in through the uncurtained windows, she sat with her profile, cameo-like (or like perhaps to the head on a postage stamp) against the dark oak walls of her music-room, and entranced herself and her listeners, if there were people to dinner, with the exquisite pathos of the first movement of the *Moonlight Sonata*. Devotedly as she worshipped the Master, whose picture hung above her Steinway Grand, she could never bring herself to believe that the two succeeding movements were on the same sublime level as the first, and besides they 'went' very much faster. But she had seriously thought, as she came down in the train today and planned her fresh activities at home of trying to master them, so that she could get through their intricacies with tolerable accuracy. Until then, she would assuredly stop at the end of the first movement in these moonlit seances, and say that the other two were more like morning and afternoon.

E. F. Benson, *Queen Lucia*

If you fear you're the only one who finds parties stressful:

At the same time, it seemed to Mr Denham as if a thousand softly padded doors had closed between him and the street outside. A fine mist, the etherealised essence of the fog, hung visibly in the wide and rather empty space of the drawing-room, all silver where the candles were grouped on the tea-table, and ruddy again in the firelight. With the omnibuses and cabs still running in his head, and his body still tingling with his quick walk along the streets and in and out of traffic and foot-passengers, this drawing-room seemed very remote and still; and the faces of the elderly people were mellowed, at some distance from each other, and had a bloom on them owing to the fact that the air in the drawing-room was thickened by blue grains of mist. Mr Denham had come in as Mr Fortescue, the eminent novelist, reached the middle of a very long sentence. He kept this suspended while the newcomer sat down, and Mrs Hilbery deftly joined the severed parts by leaning towards him and remarking:

'Now, what would you do if you were married to an engineer, and had to live in Manchester, Mr Denham?'

'Surely she could learn Persian,' broke in a thin, elderly gentleman. 'Is there no retired schoolmaster or man of letters in Manchester with whom she could read Persian?'

'A cousin of ours has married and gone to live in Manchester,' Katharine explained. Mr Denham muttered something, which was indeed all that was required of him, and the novelist went on where he had left off. Privately, Mr Denham cursed himself very sharply for having exchanged the freedom of the street for this sophisticated drawing-room, where, among other disagreeables, he certainly would not appear at his best. He glanced round him, and saw that, save for Katharine, they were all over forty, the only consolation being that Mr Fortescue was a considerable celebrity, so that to-morrow one might be glad to have met him.

Virginia Woolf, *Night and Day*

If you wonder whether you're the only one who doesn't get carried away on New Year's Eve:

No one ever regarded the First of January with indifference. It is that from which all date their time, and count upon what is left. It is the nativity of our common Adam.

Of all sounds of all bells — (bells, the music nighest bordering upon heaven) — most solemn and touching is the peal which rings out the Old Year. I never hear it without a gathering-up of my mind to a concentration of all the images that have been diffused over the past twelvemonth; all I have done or suffered, performed or neglected — in that regretted time. I begin to know its worth, as when a person dies. It takes a personal colour; nor was it a poetical flight in a contemporary, when he exclaimed —

I saw the skirts of the departing Year.

It is no more than what in sober sadness every one of us seems to be conscious of, in that awful leave-taking. I am sure I felt it, and all felt it with me, last night; though some of my companions affected rather to manifest an exhilaration at the birth of the coming year, than any very tender regrets for the decease of its predecessor. But I am none of those who –

Welcome the coming, speed the parting guest.

I am naturally, beforehand, shy of novelties; new books, new faces, new years, from some mental twist which makes it difficult in me to face the prospective.

Charles Lamb, 'New Year's Eve'

BOOKS
AND
READING

If anyone tells you that you spend too much time reading books:

For books are not absolutely dead things, but do contain a potency of life in them to be as active as that soul was whose progeny they are; nay, they do preserve as in a vial the purest efficacy and extraction of that living intellect that bred them. I know they are as lively, and as vigorously productive, as those fabulous dragon's teeth; and being sown up and down, may chance to spring up armed men. And yet, on the other hand, unless wariness be used, as good almost kill a man as kill a good book. Who kills a man kills a reasonable creature, God's image; but he who destroys a good book, kills reason itself, kills the image of God, as it were in the eye. Many a man lives a burden to the earth; but a good book is the precious life-blood of a master spirit, embalmed and treasured up on purpose to a life beyond life.

John Milton, *Areopagitica*

If you need any help arguing for the existence of public libraries:

There was a library in Coketown, to which general access was easy. Mr Gradgrind greatly tormented his mind about what the people read in this library: a point whereon little rivers of tabular statements periodically flowed into the howling ocean of tabular statements, which no diver ever got to any depth in and came up sane. It was a disheartening circumstance, but a melancholy fact, that even these readers persisted in wondering. They wondered about human nature, human passions, human hopes and fears, the struggles, triumphs and defeats, the cares and joys and sorrows, the lives and deaths of common men and women! They sometimes, after fifteen hours' work, sat down to read mere fables about men and women, more or less like themselves, and about children, more or less like their own. They took De Foe to their bosoms, instead of Euclid, and seemed to be on the whole more comforted by Goldsmith than by Cocker. Mr Gradgrind was for ever working, in print and out of print, at this eccentric sum, and he never could make out how it yielded this unaccountable product.

Charles Dickens, *Hard Times*

If you wonder whether it's acceptable to abandon a book before you've finished it:

Some books are to be tasted, others to be swallowed, and some few to be chewed and digested; that is, some books are to be read only in parts; others to be read, but not curiously; and some few to be read wholly, and with diligence and attention.

Francis Bacon, *The Essays or Counsels, Civil and Moral*

If you are tired of people criticising your love of fiction:

Although our productions have afforded more extensive and unaffected pleasure than those of any other literary corporation in the world, no species of composition has been so much decried. From pride, ignorance, or fashion, our foes are almost as many as our readers. And while the abilities of the nine-hundredth abridger of the History of England, or of the man who collects and publishes in a volume some dozen lines of Milton, Pope, and Prior, with a paper from the Spectator, and a chapter from Sterne, are eulogised by a thousand pens – there seems almost a general wish of decrying the capacity and undervaluing the labour of the novelist, and of slighting the performances which have only genius, wit, and taste to recommend them. 'I am no novel-reader – I seldom look into novels – Do not imagine that I often read novels – It is really very well for a novel.' Such is the common cant. 'And what are you reading, Miss –?' 'Oh! It is only a novel!' replies the young lady, while she lays down her book with affected indifference, or momentary shame. 'It is only Cecilia, or Camilla, or Belinda'; or, in short, only some work in which the greatest powers of the mind are displayed, in which the most thorough knowledge of human nature, the happiest delineation of its varieties, the liveliest effusions of wit and humour, are conveyed to the world in the best-chosen language. Now, had the same young lady been engaged with a volume of the Spectator, instead of such a work, how proudly would she have produced the book, and told its name; though the chances must be against her being occupied by any part of that voluminous publication, of which either the matter or manner would not disgust a young person of taste: the substance of its papers so often consisting in the statement of improbable circumstances, unnatural characters, and topics of conversation which no longer concern anyone living; and their language, too, frequently so coarse as to give no very favourable idea of the age that could endure it.

Jane Austen, *Northanger Abbey*

If you are struggling to understand a piece of avant-garde literature:

Great indulgence is due to the errors of original writers, who, quitting the beaten track which others have travelled, make daring incursions into unexplored regions of invention, and boldly strike into the pathless sublime: it is no wonder if they are often bewildered, sometimes benighted; yet surely it is more eligible to partake the pleasure and the toil of their adventures, than still to follow the cautious steps of timid imitators through trite and common roads. Genius is of a bold enterprising nature, ill adapted to the formal restraints of critic institutions, or indeed to lay down to itself rules of nice discretion.

Elizabeth Montagu, *An Essay on the Writings and Genius of Shakespeare*

If you are being mocked for studying the classics:

It is not in vain that the farmer remembers and repeats the few Latin words which he has heard. Men sometimes speak as if the study of the classics would at length make way for more modern and practical studies; but the adventurous student will always study classics, in whatever language they may be written and however ancient they may be. For what are the classics but the noblest recorded thoughts of man? They are the only oracles which are not decayed, and there are such answers to the most modern inquiry in them as Delphi and Dodona never gave. We might as well omit to study Nature because she is old. To read well, that is, to read true books in a true spirit, is a noble exercise, and one that will task the reader more than any exercise which the customs of the day esteem.

Henry David Thoreau, *Walden*

If you want to understand why poetry is so uniquely powerful:

Poetry turns all things to loveliness; it exalts the beauty of that which is most beautiful, and it adds beauty to that which is most deformed; it marries exultation and horror, grief and pleasure, eternity and change; it subdues to union under its light yoke all irreconcilable things. It transmutes all that it touches, and every form moving within the radiance of its presence is changed by wondrous sympathy to an incarnation of the spirit which it breathes: its secret alchemy turns to potable gold the poisonous waters which flow from death through life; it strips the veil of familiarity from the world, and lays bare the naked and sleeping beauty, which is the spirit of its forms.

Percy Bysshe Shelley, 'A Defence of Poetry'

TRAVEL

If you are preparing for a holiday and need help with your packing strategy:

'Always before beginning to pack,' my Uncle would say, 'make a list.'

He was a methodical man.

'Take a piece of paper' – he always began at the beginning – 'put down on it everything you can possibly require, then go over it and see that it contains nothing you can possibly do without. Imagine yourself in bed; what have you got on? Very well, put it down – together with a change. You get up; what do you do? Wash yourself. What do you wash yourself with? Soap; put down soap. Go on till you have finished. Then take your clothes. Begin at your feet; what do you wear on your feet? Boots, shoes, socks; put them down. Work up till you get to your head. What else do you want besides clothes? A little brandy; put it down. A corkscrew, put it down. Put down everything, then you don't forget anything.'

That is the plan he always pursued himself. The list made, he would go over it carefully, as he always advised, to see that he had forgotten nothing. Then he would go over it again, and strike out everything it was possible to dispense with.

Then he would lose the list.

Jerome K. Jerome, *Three Men on the Bummel*

If you need to calculate your speed while travelling:

And so it happened that an hour or so later I found myself in the corner of a first-class carriage flying along en route for Exeter, while Sherlock Holmes, with his sharp, eager face framed in his ear-flapped travelling-cap, dipped rapidly into the bundle of fresh papers which he had procured at Paddington. We had left Reading far behind us before he thrust the last one of them under the seat, and offered me his cigar-case.

'We are going well,' said he, looking out the window and glancing at his watch. 'Our rate at present is fifty-three and a half miles an hour.'

'I have not observed the quarter-mile posts,' said I.

'Nor have I. But the telegraph posts upon this line are sixty yards apart, and the calculation is a simple one.'

Arthur Conan Doyle, *The Memoirs of Sherlock Holmes*

If you are keen to learn new accents but find the variety of sounds overwhelming:

HIGGINS: Well, I think that's the whole show.

PICKERING: It's really amazing. I haven't taken half of it in, you know.

HIGGINS: Would you like to go over any of it again?

PICKERING: No, thank you; not now. I'm quite done up for this morning.

HIGGINS: Tired of listening to sounds?

PICKERING: Yes. It's a fearful strain. I rather fancied myself because I can pronounce twenty-four distinct vowel sounds; but your hundred and thirty beat me. I can't hear a bit of difference between most of them.

HIGGINS: Oh, that comes with practice. You hear no difference at first; but you keep on listening, and presently you find they're all as different as A from B.

George Bernard Shaw, *Pygmalion*

If you are finding it difficult to get your point across when you are travelling:

At last I ventured a story myself; and vast was the success of it. Not right off, of course, for the native of those islands does not, as a rule, dissolve upon the early applications of a humorous thing; but the fifth time I told it, they began to crack in places; the eighth time I told it, they began to crumble; at the twelfth repetition they fell apart in chunks; and at the fifteenth they disintegrated, and I got a broom and swept them up. This language is figurative. Those islanders – well, they are slow pay at first, in the matter of return for your investment of effort, but in the end they make the pay of all other nations poor and small by contrast.

Mark Twain, *A Connecticut Yankee
in King Arthur's Court*

If you fear that a riverside holiday will be boring:

'I beg your pardon,' said the Mole, pulling himself together with an effort. 'You must think me very rude; but all this is so new to me. So – this – is – a – River!'

'THE River,' corrected the Rat.

'And you really live by the river? What a jolly life!'

'By it and with it and on it and in it,' said the Rat. 'It's brother and sister to me, and aunts, and company, and food and drink, and (naturally) washing. It's my world, and I don't want any other. What it hasn't got is not worth having, and what it doesn't know is not worth knowing. Lord! the times we've had together! Whether in winter or summer, spring or autumn, it's always got its fun and its excitements. When the floods are on in February, and my cellars and basement are brimming with drink that's no good to me, and the brown water runs by my best bedroom window; or again when it all drops away and, shows patches of mud that smells like plum-cake, and the rushes and weed clog the channels, and I can potter about dry shod over most of the bed of it and find fresh food to eat, and things careless people have dropped out of boats!'

'But isn't it a bit dull at times?' the Mole ventured to ask. 'Just you and the river, and no one else to pass a word with?'

'No one else to – well, I mustn't be hard on you,' said the Rat with forbearance. 'You're new to it, and of course you don't know. The bank is so crowded nowadays that many people are moving away altogether: O no, it isn't what it used to be, at all. Otters, kingfishers, dabchicks, moorhens, all of them about all day long and always wanting you to DO something – as if a fellow had no business of his own to attend to!'

Kenneth Grahame, *The Wind in the Willows*

If you are worried that capital cities are dangerous places:

'So you were never in London before?' said Mr Wemmick to me.

'No,' said I.

'I was new here once,' said Mr Wemmick. 'Rum to think of now!'

'You are well acquainted with it now?'

'Why, yes,' said Mr Wemmick. 'I know the moves of it.'

'Is it a very wicked place?' I asked, more for the sake of saying something than for information.

'You may get cheated, robbed, and murdered in London. But there are plenty of people anywhere, who'll do that for you.'

Charles Dickens, *Great Expectations*

If, while travelling in Ireland, you are tempted to try the local spirits:

Let all English be recommended to be very careful of whiskey, which experience teaches to be a very deleterious drink. Natives say that it is wholesome, and may be sometimes seen to use it with impunity; but the whiskey-fever is naturally more fatal to strangers than inhabitants of the country; and whereas an Irishman will sometimes imbibe a half-dozen tumblers of the poison, two glasses will be often found to cause headaches, heartburns, and fevers to a person newly arrived in the country.

William Makepeace Thackeray,
The Irish Sketch Book

If you are wondering what to take with you on a hiking holiday in Scotland:

The Highlands can be enjoyed in the utmost simplicity; and the best preparations are — money to a moderate extent in one's pocket, a knapsack containing a spare shirt and a toothbrush, and a courage that does not fear to breast the steep of the hill, and to encounter the pelting of a Highland shower. No man knows a country till he has walked through it; he then tastes the sweets and the bitters of it.

Alexander Smith, *A Summer in Skye*

If you are travelling in Germany and find the language frustratingly hard to get to grips with:

There are ten parts of speech, and they are all troublesome. An average sentence, in a German newspaper, is a sublime and impressive curiosity; it occupies a quarter of a column; it contains all the ten parts of speech – not in regular order, but mixed; it is built mainly of compound words constructed by the writer on the spot, and not to be found in any dictionary – six or seven words compacted into one, without joint or seam – that is, without hyphens; it treats of fourteen or fifteen different subjects, each enclosed in a parenthesis of its own, with here and there extra parentheses, making pens within pens: finally, all the parentheses and reparentheses are massed together between a couple of king-parentheses, one of which is placed in the first line of the majestic sentence and the other in the middle of the last line of it – *after which comes the verb*, and you find out for the first time what the man has been talking about; and after the verb – merely by way of ornament, as far as I can make out – the writer shovels in '*haben sind gewesen gehabt haven geworden sein*,' or words to that effect, and the monument is finished. I suppose that this closing hurrah is in the nature of the flourish to a man's signature – not necessary, but pretty. German books are easy enough to read when you hold them before the looking-glass or stand on your head – so as to reverse the construction – but I think that to learn to read and understand a German newspaper is a thing which must always remain an impossibility to a foreigner.

Mark Twain, *A Tramp Abroad*

If you would like to move to the countryside but fear your friends will stop visiting you:

I had more visitors while I lived in the woods than at any other period in my life; I mean that I had some. I met several there under more favorable circumstances than I could anywhere else. But fewer came to see me on trivial business. In this respect, my company was winnowed by my mere distance from town. I had withdrawn so far within the great ocean of solitude, into which the rivers of society empty, that for the most part, so far as my needs were concerned, only the finest sediment was deposited around me. Beside, there were wafted to me evidences of unexplored and uncultivated continents on the other side.

Henry David Thoreau, *Walden*

THE
NATURAL
WORLD

If you've been invited for an early morning walk, and need a little encouragement to leave the warm comfort of your bed:

There was a feeling of freshness and vigour in the very streets; and when I got free of the town, when my foot was on the sands and my face towards the broad, bright bay, no language can describe the effect of the deep, clear azure of the sky and ocean, the bright morning sunshine on the semicircular barrier of craggy cliffs surmounted by green swelling hills, and on the smooth, wide sands, and the low rocks out at sea – looking, with their clothing of weeds and moss, like little grass-grown islands – and above all, on the brilliant, sparkling waves. And then, the unspeakable purity – and freshness of the air! There was just enough heat to enhance the value of the breeze, and just enough wind to keep the whole sea in motion, to make the waves come bounding to the shore, foaming and sparkling, as if wild with glee. Nothing else was stirring – no living creature was visible besides myself.

My footsteps were the first to press the firm, unbroken sands; – nothing before had trampled them since last night's flowing tide had obliterated the deepest marks of yesterday, and left them fair and even, except where the subsiding water had left behind it the traces of dimpled pools and little running streams.

Anne Brontë, *Agnes Grey*

If you are dreading the winter cold:

As I am what the men of the world, if they knew such a man, would call a whimsical mortal, I have various sources of pleasure and enjoyment, which are, in a manner, peculiar to myself, or some here and there such other out-of-the-way person. Such is the peculiar pleasure I take in the season of winter, more than the rest of the year. This, I believe, may be partly owing to my misfortunes giving my mind a melancholy cast: but there is something even in the

'Mighty tempest, and the hoary waste
Abrupt and deep, stretch'd o'er the buried earth,' –

which raises the mind to a serious sublimity, favourable to everything great and noble. There is scarcely any earthly object gives me more – I do not know if I should call it pleasure – but something which exalts me, something which enraptures me – than to walk in the sheltered side of a wood, or high plantation, in a cloudy winter-day, and hear the stormy wind howling among the trees, and raving over the plain.

Robert Burns, 'To Robert Riddel, Esq. of Glenriddel'

If you need some advice on how to lay out your garden:

The garden is best to be square, encompassed on all the four sides with a stately arched hedge. The arches to be upon pillars of carpenter's work, of some ten foot high and six foot broad; and the spaces between of the same dimension with the breadth of the arch. Over the arches let there be an entire hedge, of some four foot high, framed also upon carpenter's work; and upon the upper hedge, over every arch, a little turret, with a belly, enough to receive a cage of birds; and over every space between the arches some other little figure, with broad plates of round coloured glass, gilt, for the sun to play upon. But this hedge I intend to be raised upon a bank, not steep, but gently slope, of some six foot, set all with flowers. Also I understand, that this square of the garden should not be the whole breadth of the ground, but to leave, on either side, ground enough for diversity of side alleys; unto which the two covert alleys of the green may deliver you. But there must be no alleys with hedges at either end of this great enclosure: not at the hither end, for letting your prospect upon this fair hedge from the green; nor at the further end, for letting your prospect from the hedge, through the arches upon the heath.

Francis Bacon, 'Of Gardens'

If you are worried that your garden isn't neat enough:

He began to walk about, looking up in the trees and at the walls and bushes with a thoughtful expression.

'I wouldn't want to make it look like a gardener's garden, all clipped an' spick an' span, would you?' he said. 'It's nicer like this with things runnin' wild, an' swingin' an' catchin' hold of each other.'

'Don't let us make it tidy,' said Mary anxiously. 'It wouldn't seem like a secret garden if it was tidy.'

Frances Hodgson Burnett, *The Secret Garden*

If you need to keep donkey-riders (or any other trespassers) off your lawn:

'Good day, sir,' said my aunt, 'and good-bye! Good day to you, too, ma'am,' said my aunt, turning suddenly upon his sister. 'Let me see you ride a donkey over my green again, and as sure as you have a head upon your shoulders, I'll knock your bonnet off, and tread upon it!'

It would require a painter, and no common painter too, to depict my aunt's face as she delivered herself of this very unexpected sentiment, and Miss Murdstone's face as she heard it. But the manner of the speech, no less than the matter, was so fiery, that Miss Murdstone, without a word in answer, discreetly put her arm through her brother's, and walked haughtily out of the cottage; my aunt remaining in the window looking after them; prepared, I have no doubt, in case of the donkey's reappearance, to carry her threat into instant execution.

Charles Dickens, *David Copperfield*

If people think you're crazy because you talk to your plants:

'O Tiger-lily,' said Alice, addressing herself to one that was waving gracefully about in the wind, 'I *wish* you could talk!'

'We *can* talk,' said the Tiger-lily, 'when there's anybody worth talking to.'

Alice was so astonished that she couldn't speak for a minute: it quite seemed to take her breath away. At length, as the Tiger-lily only went on waving about, she spoke again, in a timid voice — almost in a whisper. 'And can *all* the flowers talk?'

'As well as you can,' said the Tiger-lily. 'And a great deal louder.'

'It isn't manners for us to begin, you know,' said the Rose, 'and I really was wondering when you'd speak! Said I to myself, "Her face has got *some* sense in it, though it's not a clever one!" Still you're the right colour, and that goes a long way.'

'I don't care about the colour,' the Tiger-lily remarked. 'If only her petals curled up a little more, she'd be all right.'

Lewis Carroll, *Through the Looking-Glass, and What Alice Found There*

If your friends don't understand why you enjoy birdwatching:

Why keep pets when every wild, free hawk that passed overhead in the air was mine? I joyed in his swift, careless flight, in the throw of his pinions, in his rush over the elms and miles of woodland; it was happiness to see his unchecked life. What more beautiful than the sweep and curve of his going through the azure sky?

Richard Jefferies, 'Hours of Spring'

If you are wondering whether the songs of birds can be written down as music:

From what follows, it will appear that neither owls nor cuckoos keep to one note. A friend remarks that many (most) of his owls hoot in B flat: but that one went almost half a note below A. The pipe he tried their notes by was a common half-crown pitch-pipe, such as masters use for tuning of harpsichords; it was the common London pitch.

A neighbour of mine, who is said to have a nice ear, remarks that the owls about this village hoot in three different keys, in G flat, or F sharp, in B flat and A flat. He heard two hooting to each other, the one in A flat, and the other in B flat. Query: Do these different notes proceed from different species, or only from various individuals? The same person finds upon trial that the note of the cuckoo (of which we have but one species) varies in different individuals; for, about Selborne wood, he found they were mostly in D: he heard two sing together, the one in D, the other in D sharp, who made a disagreeable concert: he afterwards heard one in D sharp, and about Wolmer-forest some in C. As to nightingales, he says that their notes are so short, and their transitions so rapid, that he cannot well ascertain their key. Perhaps in a cage, and in a room, their notes may be more distinguishable. This person has tried to settle the notes of a swift, and of several other small birds, but cannot bring them to any criterion.

Gilbert White, *The Natural History and Antiquities of Selborne*

LIFE'S BIG QUESTIONS

If you wonder just how far an optimistic outlook can take you in life:

At this point they came in sight of thirty forty windmills that there are on plain, and as soon as Don Quixote saw them he said to his squire, 'Fortune is arranging matters for us better than we could have shaped our desires ourselves, for look there, friend Sancho Panza, where thirty or more monstrous giants present themselves, all of whom I mean to engage in battle and slay, and with whose spoils we shall begin to make our fortunes; for this is righteous warfare, and it is God's good service to sweep so evil a breed from off the face of the earth.'

'What giants?' said Sancho Panza.

'Those thou seest there,' answered his master, 'with the long arms, and some have them nearly two leagues long.'

'Look, your worship,' said Sancho; 'what we see there are not giants but windmills, and what seem to be their arms are the sails that turned by the wind make the millstone go.'

'It is easy to see,' replied Don Quixote, 'that thou art not used to this business of adventures; those are giants; and if thou art afraid, away with thee out of this and betake thyself to prayer while I engage them in fierce and unequal combat.'

So saying, he gave the spur to his steed Rocinante, heedless of the cries his squire Sancho sent after him, warning him that most certainly they were windmills and not giants he was going to attack. He, however, was so positive they were giants that he neither heard the cries of Sancho, nor perceived, near as he was, what they were, but made at them shouting, 'Fly not, cowards and vile beings, for a single knight attacks you.'

A slight breeze at this moment sprang up, and the great sails began to move, seeing which Don Quixote exclaimed, 'Though ye flourish more arms than the giant Briareus, ye have to reckon with me.'

So saying, and commending himself with all his heart to his lady Dulcinea, imploring her to support him in such a peril, with lance in rest and covered by his buckler, he charged at Rocinante's fullest gallop and fell upon the first mill that stood in front of him; but as he drove his lance-point into the sail the wind whirled it round with such force that it shivered the lance to pieces, sweeping with it horse and rider, who went rolling over on the plain, in a sorry condition. Sancho hastened to his assistance as fast as his ass could go, and when he came up found him unable to move, with such a shock had Rocinante fallen with him.

'God bless me!' said Sancho, 'did I not tell your worship to mind what you were about, for they were only windmills? and no one could have made any mistake about it but one who had something of the same kind in his head.'

'Hush, friend Sancho,' replied Don Quixote, 'the fortunes of war more than any other are liable to frequent fluctuations; and moreover I think, and it is the truth, that that same sage Friston who carried off my study and books, has turned these giants into mills in order to rob me of the glory of vanquishing them, such is the enmity he bears me; but in the end his wicked arts will avail but little against my good sword.'

Miguel de Cervantes, *Don Quixote*

If you are overwhelmed by the need to laugh and cry at the same time:

We are to consider how much our souls are oftentimes agitated with divers passions. And as they say that in our bodies there is a congregation of divers humours, of which that is the sovereign which, according to the complexion we are of, is commonly most predominant in us: so, though the soul have in it divers motions to give it agitation, yet must there of necessity be one to overrule all the rest, though not with so necessary and absolute a dominion but that through the flexibility and inconstancy of the soul, those of less authority may upon occasion reassume their place and make a little sally in turn. Thence it is, that we see not only children, who innocently obey and follow nature, often laugh and cry at the same thing, but not one of us can boast, what journey soever he may have in hand that he has the most set his heart upon, but when he comes to part with his family and friends, he will find something that troubles him within; and though he refrain his tears yet he puts foot in the stirrup with a sad and cloudy countenance.

Michel de Montaigne, 'That We Laugh
and Cry for the Same Thing'

If you are accused of being too idealistic:

If ever men might lawfully dream awake, and give utterance to their wildest visions without dread of laughter or scorn on the part of the audience, – yes, and speak of earthly happiness, for themselves and mankind, as an object to be hopefully striven for, and probably attained, we who made that little semicircle round the blazing fire were those very men. We had left the rusty iron framework of society behind us; we had broken through many hindrances that are powerful enough to keep most people on the weary treadmill of the established system, even while they feel its irksomeness almost as intolerable as we did. We had stepped down from the pulpit; we had flung aside the pen; we had shut up the ledger; we had thrown off that sweet, bewitching, enervating indolence, which is better, after all, than most of the enjoyments within mortal grasp. It was our purpose – a generous one, certainly, and absurd, no doubt, in full proportion with its generosity – to give up whatever we had heretofore attained, for the sake of showing mankind the example of a life governed by other than the false and cruel principles on which human society has all along been based.

And, first of all, we had divorced ourselves from pride, and were striving to supply its place with familiar love. We meant to lessen the labouring man's great burden of toil, by performing our due share of it at the cost of our own thews and sinews. We sought our profit by mutual aid, instead of wresting it by the strong hand from an enemy, or filching it craftily from those less shrewd than ourselves (if, indeed, there were any such in New England), or winning it by selfish competition with a neighbour; in one or another of which fashions every son of woman both perpetrates and suffers his share of the common evil, whether he chooses it or no. And, as the basis of our institution, we purposed to offer up the earnest toil of our bodies, as a prayer no less than an effort for the advancement of our race.

Therefore, if we built splendid castles (phalansteries perhaps they might be more fitly called), and pictured beautiful scenes, among the fervid coals of the hearth around which we were clustering, and if all went to rack with the crumbling embers and have never since arisen out of the ashes, let us take to ourselves no shame. In my own behalf, I rejoice that I could once think better of the world's improvability than it deserved. It is a mistake into which men seldom fall twice in a lifetime; or, if so, the rarer and higher is the nature that can thus magnanimously persist in error.

Nathaniel Hawthorne, *The Blithedale Romance*

If you wonder whether other planets are guided by different moral rules to the ones we know:

'Reason and justice grip the remotest and the loneliest star. Look at those stars. Don't they look as if they were single diamonds and sapphires? Well, you can imagine any mad botany or geology you please. Think of forests of adamant with leaves of brilliants. Think the moon is a blue moon, a single elephantine sapphire. But don't fancy that all that frantic astronomy would make the smallest difference to the reason and justice of conduct. On plains of opal, under cliffs cut out of pearl, you would still find a notice-board, "I hou shalt not steal."'

G. K. Chesterton, *The Innocence of Father Brown*

If you wonder whether it is really worth writing down your thoughts and creating something to leave behind you:

Now this to me speaks as the roll of thunder that cannot be denied — you must hear it; and how can you shut your ears to what this lark sings, this violet tells, this little grey shell writes in the curl of its spire? The bitter truth that human life is no more to the universe than that of the unnoticed hill-snail in the grass should make us think more and more highly of ourselves as human — as men — living things that think. We must look to ourselves to help ourselves. We must think ourselves into an earthly immortality. By day and by night, by years and by centuries, still striving, studying, searching to find that which shall enable us to live a fuller life upon the earth — to have a wider grasp upon its violets and loveliness, a deeper draught of the sweet-briar wind. Because my heart beats feebly to-day, my trickling pulse scarcely notating the passing of the time, so much the more do I hope that those to come in future years may see wider and enjoy fuller than I have done; and so much the more gladly would I do all that I could to enlarge the life that shall be then.

Richard Jefferies, 'Hours of Spring'

If you worry that you are not fitting in with other people's ways of life:

Some people are born with a vital and responsive energy. It not only enables them to keep abreast of the times; it qualifies them to furnish in their own personality a good bit of the motive power to the mad pace. They are fortunate beings. They do not need to apprehend the significance of things. They do not grow weary nor miss step, nor do they fall out of rank and sink by the wayside to be left contemplating the moving procession.

Ah! that moving procession that has left me by the road-side! Its fantastic colours are more brilliant and beautiful than the sun on the undulating waters. What matter if souls and bodies are failing beneath the feet of the ever-pressing multitude! It moves with the majestic rhythm of the spheres. Its discordant clashes sweep upward in one harmonious tone that blends with the music of other worlds – to complete God's orchestra.

It is greater than the stars – that moving procession of human energy; greater than the palpitating earth and the things growing thereon. Oh! I could weep at being left by the wayside; left with the grass and the clouds and a few dumb animals. True, I feel at home in the society of these symbols of life's immutability. In the procession I should feel the crushing feet, the clashing discords, the ruthless hands and stifling breath. I could not hear the rhythm of the march.

Salve! ye dumb hearts. Let us be still and wait by the roadside.

Kate Chopin, *The Awakening*

If you fear you are alone in feeling unsure of your place and purpose in the universe:

I don't require you to fall in love with my boy, but I do think you might try and understand him. You are nearer his age, and if you let yourself go I am sure you are sensible. You might help me. He has known so few women, and you have the time. You stop here several weeks, I suppose? But let yourself go. You are inclined to get muddled, if I may judge from last night. Let yourself go. Pull out from the depths those thoughts that you do not understand, and spread them out in the sunlight and know the meaning of them. By understanding George you may learn to understand yourself. It will be good for both of you.'

To this extraordinary speech Lucy found no answer.

'I only know what it is that's wrong with him; not why it is.'

'And what is it?' asked Lucy fearfully, expecting some harrowing tale.

'The old trouble; things won't fit.'

'What things?'

'The things of the universe. It is quite true. They don't.'

'Oh, Mr Emerson, whatever do you mean?'

In his ordinary voice, so that she scarcely realised he was quoting poetry, he said:

> '"From far, from eve and morning,
>   And yon twelve-winded sky,
>   The stuff of life to knit me
>   Blew hither: here am I"

George and I both know this, but why does it distress him? We know that we come from the winds, and that we shall return to them; that all life is perhaps a knot, a tangle, a blemish in the eternal smoothness. But why should this make us unhappy? Let us rather love one another, and work and rejoice. I don't believe in this world sorrow.'

Miss Honeychurch assented.

'Then make my boy think like us. Make him realise that by the side of the everlasting Why there is a Yes — a transitory Yes if you like, but a Yes.'

E. M. Forster, *A Room with a View*

If you never seem to have enough time to get things done:

Alice sighed wearily. 'I think you might do something better with the time,' she said, 'than waste it in asking riddles that have no answers.'

'If you knew Time as well as I do,' said the Hatter, 'you wouldn't talk about wasting it. It's him.'

'I don't know what you mean,' said Alice.

'Of course you don't!' the Hatter said, tossing his head contemptuously. 'I dare say you never even spoke to Time!'

'Perhaps not,' Alice cautiously replied: 'but I know I have to beat time when I learn music.'

'Ah! that accounts for it,' said the Hatter. 'He won't stand beating. Now, if you only kept on good terms with him, he'd do almost anything you liked with the clock. For instance, suppose it were nine o'clock in the morning, just time to begin lessons: you'd only have to whisper a hint to Time, and round goes the clock in a twinkling! Half-past one, time for dinner!'

Lewis Carroll, *Alice's Adventures in Wonderland*

INDEX OF
AUTHORS

185

POETRY FIRST AID KIT

Poems for Everyday Dilemmas, Decisions and Emergencies

ABBIE HEADON

POETRY FIRST AID KIT
Poems for Everyday Dilemmas, Decisions and Emergencies

Abbie Headon

ISBN: 978 1 84953 465 9
Hardback
£9.99

Whether your problem is an everyday conundrum or a life-changing decision, the world of poetry is sure to provide an inspiring answer.

Seek a solution within these stanzas and let the rhymes and rhythms help you resolve the dilemmas in your life.

'Offering enlightenment, solace and humour, she offers an original way to gain perspective simply by dipping in to this volume for kernels of poetic wisdom that offer consolation for life's vicissitudes.'

GOOD BOOK GUIDE

POETRY FIRST AID KIT

PRAYER FIRST AID KIT

Prayers for Everyday Dilemmas,
Decisions and Emergencies

VICTORIA LORENZATO

PRAYER FIRST AID KIT
Prayers for Everyday Dilemmas, Decisions and Emergencies

Victoria Lorenzato

ISBN: 978 1 84953 734 6
Hardback
£8.99

Whether you're in need of advice, comfort or an outlet for joy in happy moments, the world of prayer can offer a safe and reassuring place to express your feelings and search for answers.

Let this collection of inspiring and illuminating prayers for every occasion help you resolve the dilemmas in your life.

Have you enjoyed this book?
If so, why not write a review on your favourite website?

If you're interested in finding out more about our
books, find us on Facebook at
Summersdale Publishers and follow us
on Twitter at **@Summersdale**.

Thanks very much for buying this Summersdale book.

www.summersdale.com